Introduction

A GARDEN OF POEMS from the Salesian Collection is the sixth of our hardbound series. It is a thoughtful selection of inspirational, and meaningful poems.

This type of poetry sustains our hearts and souls and offers guidance and encouragement in the face of every day living.

Not all of the poets in this anthology have been published. However, many of their works will become favorites of the reader because of what they have to say.

Some are simple, but rich and full in content. The variety is such, that readers from all walks of life will find their own special treasures in this collection.

We are ever grateful for the generous cooperation of the poets and publishing companies in permitting us to draw upon the wonderful wealth of wisdom and inspiration from their poetry.

Salesian Missions wishes to thank those who have given their kind permission to reprint material included in this book. Every effort has been made to give proper acknowledgements. Any omissions or errors are deeply regretted, and the publisher, upon notification, will be pleased to make necessary corrections in subsequent editions.

ACKNOWLEDGEMENTS: "What God Hath Promised" by Annie Johnson Flint, "O God, Whose Love Is Over All" by John Haynes Holmes, "A Sun-Day Hymn" by Oliver Wendell Holmes, "My Daily Prayer" by Grenville Kleiser, "Love Thyself Last" by Ella Wheeler Wilcox, are reprinted from MASTERPIECES OF RELIGIOUS VERSE, 1948, edited by James Dalton Morrison, by permission of Harper and Row. "Dawn to Dusk, A Touch of Love" and "Make Me a Channel, Lord", by Alice Joyce Davidson with permission of author.

A Garden of Poems
of Poems

from the Salesian Collection

Compiled and Edited by
Sara Tarascio

Illustrated by
Marion L. Quimby
Paul Scully
Frank Massa

CONTENTS

The Art of Living 6

Never Hopeless 7

In Thankfulness 8

Plant and Harvest Love 10

Tall in God's Love 11

Today and Tomorrow 13

Trust 14

Lay Your Burdens Down ... 15

A Sun-day Hymn 16

Faith looks 18

My Goal 19

Wings Against the Sun 21

Life's Great Sea 22

Be Happy Recipe 24

God's Eternal Love 25

God's Tender Care 26

Special Thoughts 27

God's Sunshine Was There .. 28

A Prayer 29

There's Always a
    Silver Lining 30

My Companion 31

Morning Renewal 32

"Just One Thing" 33

The Whisper of Love 34

Look Up! 36

Within His Care 37

Prayer for Faith 38

Where Faith Begins 39

Beyond Our Asking 40

Love Thyself Last 42

God's Love 43

Live Today 44

Let not your heart 45

Sound of Love 46

Believe and Pray 47

God Is Faithful 48

Dawn to Dusk 50

Yesterday 51

Good Shepherd 52

Open My Eyes 54

Nobody Walks Alone 55

The Golden Years 56

Tuning 58

The Search 59

God's Love Lingers On 60

Great Hearts 62

Trust 63

God's Rope 64

God! 65

What More Can You Ask ... 66

Hold On 68

In Him You'll Find Peace ... 69

Daybreak 70

The Gentle Shepherd 71

A Sinner's Promise 72

Stepping Stones 74

Save Room in Your Heart ... 75

How to Find Happiness 76

Release 78

Delay 79

Did Someone Wake
    at Dawn? 80

Thanks for Today 81

Morning Prayer 82

Exalted Happiness 84

Take Time 85

Limitations 86

We Are All Kin 87

Praise the Lord 88

My Worry 89

Quiet Peace 90

Made for You 91

Perfect Trust 92

My Daily Prayer 94

Love is an Attitude 95

I Have Been Blessed 96

The Hand of the
    Heavenly Host 99

Sunshine and Music 100

God Give Me Joy 101

A Little Candle 102

Oh God, Whose Love
    Is Over All 103

I Have Found Such Joy 104

Never Borrow Sorrow
    from Tomorrow 105

Live with Faith 106

Thy Will Be Done 108

Endurance 110

What God Hath Promised .. 111

Do What You Can 112

God's Creation 113

Never Alone 115

A Quiet Time 116

Somebody's Smile 117

God's Touch of Wonder 118

Waymarks 120

This I Know 121

All's Well 122

God's Love 123

Always Near You 124

Trust God 125

He Cares 126

Make Me a
    Channel, Lord! 128

The Art of Living

There's a special art to living,
And you need a frame of mind
That can overlook the showers,
'Til the sun begins to shine.
To develop to the fullest,
You have got to understand,
That things don't always function
In the way that they were planned.

There's a special art to living,
And the challenge must be met,
But the longer that you try it,
Why the better you will get.
Don't waste your time in waiting
For the world to come to you.
You have to climb the mountain,
To appreciate the view.

                    Grace E. Easley

Never Hopeless

As life goes on from day to day
And God is always near
There is no place for hopelessness
There is no need to fear.
Lift up your eyes, behold the skies
The bright, the dark, the dim
Whatever weather there may be
It is ordained by Him.
Do not despair because of some
Injustice done to you
Doubt not all other souls on earth
Because of one or two.
Do not condemn yourself too much
For wrongs that you have done
It may deplete your moral strength
In battles to be won.
Lift up your heart, have faith in God
And say a fervent prayer
For as you trust in Him, so He
Will keep you in His care.

James J. Metcalfe

In Thankfulness

Oh God, if I could but impart
The thankfulness that swells my heart
For each and every little thing . . .

Like color bursts announcing spring,
The shaded spots the trees have brought,
The sunshine brightening every thought . . .
The squirrels playing on my lawn,
The eventide . . . the still, new dawn . . .
The fragrant smell of brown leaves burned,
The fresh black dirt where earth is turned —

So many small things such as these
Have done so much my life to please
My whole life long would be of praise
To God, the Keeper of my days

Beverly Enderby Kimzey

9

Plant and Harvest Love

When you sow the seeds of love,
You know someday you'll reap
A Harvest of God's blessings,
Which you may share and keep.

For cells of love divide,
And then they split again,
A heavenly creation,
You may enter in.

So each day plant your garden,
Sow your seeds of love,
And when it's time for harvest,
It's multiplied above.

Nancy Gill

Tall in God's Love

A stately oak tree
So lofty and staunch
Stood with its head toward
   God;
It once was a seed,
A tiny acorn,
Placed in the heart of the
   sod.

Through shower and storm
Still upward it grew,
An out-branching, sheltering
   tree;
May we, like this oak,
Grow tall in God's love,
Undaunted by adversity.

Loise Pinkerton Fritz

Today and Tomorrow

Yesterday, today, and tomorrow . . .
Oh, how priceless the joy to belong . . .
For a time so brief on this planet . . .
With a bind in the Source that is strong . . .

So let us continue our journey . . .
And do our apprentice work well . . .
For in due course there shall be a harvest . . .
And joy in our hearts will prevail . . .

For while it is true we are masters . . .
With dreams and goals to achieve . . .
Let's keep aiming to reach a bit higher . . .
And with faith in our hearts to believe . . .

Soon a new door will open before us . . .
A door not opened by man . . .
For our every today and tomorrow . . .
Are a glorious part of His plan . . .

Chris Zambernard

Trust

O, strive not after the wind,
   It will elude your grasp,
Seek not to learn the why—
   Don't even ask.

Like a little child
   Walk by the Master's side
He knows your entire way
   Whatever may betide.

Lucile M. Campbell

*Verily I say unto you, except ye be
converted; and become as little
children, ye shall not enter into the
kingdom of heaven.*
           Matthew 18:3

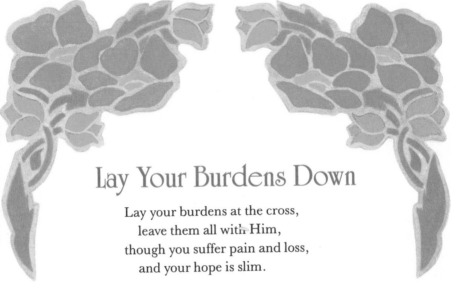

Lay Your Burdens Down

Lay your burdens at the cross,
   leave them all with Him,
though you suffer pain and loss,
   and your hope is slim.

Though your heart is dark with sorrow,
   and you're feeling low,
God will see you thru tomorrow,
   for He loves you so.

Lay your troubles in His keep,
   leave them at His door,
though the sea of life is deep,
   God is evermore.

Though each mile is full of trial,
   and your troubles grow,
God is with you all the while,
   as thru life you go.

Place yourself in Jesus' hands,
   in His gracious care,
He is Lord of all the lands,
   and He's always there.

                    Alvin Finkelstein

A Sun-Day Hymn

Lord of all being, throned afar,
Thy glory flames from sun and star;
Center and soul of every sphere,
Yet to each loving heart how near!

Sun of our life, thy quickening ray
Sheds on our path the glow of day:
Star of our hope, thy softened light
Cheers the long watches of the night.

Our midnight is thy smile withdrawn;
Our noontide is thy gracious dawn;
Our rainbow arch, thy mercy's sign:
All, save the clouds of sin, are thine.

Lord of all life, below, above,
Whose light is truth, whose warmth is
    love,
Before thy ever-blazing throne
We ask no luster of our own.

Grant us thy truth to make us free,
And kindling hearts that burn for thee,
Till all thy living altars claim
One holy light, one heavenly flame.

Oliver Wendell Holmes

Faith looks across the storm —
　　It does not doubt
Or stop to look at clouds
　　And things without.

Faith does not question why
　　When all His ways
Are hard to understand,
　　But trusts and prays.

It seeks the greatest gift
　　And asks not sight;
It does not need to see —
　　He is its light.

Above the tempest's roar
　　It hears His voice;
And, with its hands in His,
　　Faith can rejoice.

It fears no cloud, or wind
　　That it can bring;
Faith looks across the storm
　　And still can sing.

My Goal

I do not live to reach the height
That many would call fame,
But pray that I may glorify
My Blessed Saviour's name;
Each day to share the love He gives,
To be a beacon bright
Upon the path where others grope
Their way in troubled night.
Oh, how I pray for vision and
A song, when deep distress
Would overcome a troubled soul
Lost in the wilderness.
I pray to love, to reach, relieve
The ones who hunger for
The Bread of Life, the Fountain Pure,
As He waits to restore.
I pray that I can be that one
My Master would call "Friend,"
Who serves his fellowman in love,
God's kingdom to extend.

Anna Lee Edwards McAlpin

Wings Against the Sun

Forever earthbound are my feet,
Upon the rocky road ahead,
But high among the clouds, my thoughts,
And so my heart is comforted.
And if one shoulder aches, I shift
The burden to the other side,
Remembering the times I've laughed,
And not the ones in which I've cried.

Too short indeed these precious years,
To let a dream die needlessly,
Beyond tomorrow there awaits
A time and place designed for me,
And old hopes rising one by one,
Are golden wings against the sun!

Grace E. Easley

Life's Great Sea

When I am down in doldrums,
I'm drawn to the sea,
Where there the scales of nature
Seem to balance me.

The fish in their habitat,
The shells along the shore,
Provide a healthy climate,
Where I can thrive once more.

The sea gulls gang around me,
Like a group of friends,
And as I smile among them,
My sorrowful spirit ends.

As guided by an unseen force,
Which one can't see or hear,
When cast adrift on Life's Great Sea,
I *know* my God is near.

Nancy Gill

Be Happy Recipe

When the day is dreary
And you're feeling sad,
Think of something cheerful
To lift and make you glad.
If you're having problems,
You are not alone,
Life's no bed of roses,
Everyone has some.
If sorrow overtakes you,
Pray to God above,
He will not forsake you,
He comforts with His love.
Count your many blessings,
Help someone in need,
Doubt and fear will lessen,
And joy be yours indeed.

Elsie Natalie Brady

God's Eternal Love

My first thought in the morning
Is to thank God for the day,
And for the many blessings
He will send along my way.

If the faith that rests within me
Remains steadfast, firm and strong,
Then I know that peace and joy
Will be mine the whole day long.

Petty troubles will not vex me
Cause me anger or distress,
For God's loving presence guides me
To a gentle peacefulness.

Nor will I fear the future
Or what's in store for me,
For God's love will be forever
Through all eternity.

Dolores Karides

God's Tender Care

When trouble comes,
　　as it does to us all,
God is so great
　　and we are so small —
But there is nothing
　　that we need know
If we have faith
　　that wherever we go
God will be waiting
　　to help us bear
Our pain and sorrow,
　　our suffering and care —
For no pain or suffering
　　is ever too much
To yield itself
　　to God's merciful touch!

Helen Steiner Rice

Used with permission of:
The Helen Steiner Rice Foundation
Suite 2100 Atrium Two
221 E. Fourth St.
Cincinnati, OH 45202

Special Thoughts

I sent a special thought of love
    Into eternal space —
It came to me when I had done
    A kindly deed of grace —

Then back it came on wings of truth
    And chimed within my heart,
"This is the only way to build
    Life's stairway part by part."

Loreta Inman

God's Sunshine Was There

I woke in the morning
To rain on the roof,
Rain on the flowers,
Rain on the fruit.

I woke in the morning
To rain everywhere . . .
Except in my heart,
For God's sunshine was
   there.

Loise Pinkerton Fritz

A Prayer

Give us, Lord, a bit o' sun,
A bit o' work and a bit o' fun,
Give us in all the struggle and sputter,
Our daily bread and a bit o' butter,
Give us health our keep to make
And a bit to spare for other's sake
Give us, too, a bit of song,
And a tale and a book to help us along,
Give us, Lord, a chance to be
Our goodly best, brave, wise, and free,
Our goodly best for ourselves and others
Till all men learn to live as brothers.

An Old English Prayer

There's Always a Silver Lining

There's always a silver lining
Somewhere in the sky,
To bring your troubled soul new hope
And lift your spirits high.
When disappointments come your way
Accept them with a smile,
For deep down in your heart you know
They only last awhile.
Do not believe you walk alone
Because you never do.
Hold out your hand and you will find
That God is there with you.

Harold F. Mohn

My Companion

I wouldn't think of starting out
  to face the coming day,
Without a "thank you word" to God
  to help me on my way.

For when things seem uncertain,
  and my steps may falter too,
It is then I ask the Father
  for His help in what to do.

Yes, He's always there to help me
  when I stumble and I fall,
To give me aid, and pick me up,
  and guide me through it all.

What a wonderful companion,
  what a joy in life — to know,
That the Father God walks with me
  no matter where I go.

Bill Carr

Morning Renewal

Refresh me O, Lord
for the journey
that lies in this untried day!
Oh, fill me with love
and compassion
for others upon my way.

May the beautiful
Fruit of the Spirit
be abundant enough to share
with a friend
or a hungry stranger
with a heavy burden to bear.

Let me pause —
lest I go out empty
into life's turbulent street.
Oh, anoint me
to overflowing,
for the sake of the souls I'll meet!

Alice Hansche Mortenson

"Just One Thing . . ."

If I could tell you
Just one thing
That I thought worth
Remembering,

I'd tell you,
"Love! — with all your heart,
And do not stop
'Til you depart

Your earthly life
And Heav'nward soar
Where you'll be given
So much more

Of love so boundless,
Pure and true,
Stored up by God,
Returned to you."

Nancy Neff Dostie

The Whisper of Love

I cannot be sad if my Savior is near,
   He bids all my sadness depart;
I cannot be lonely, if gently I hear
   His whisper of love in my heart.

The whisper of love, soft whisper of love,
   How oft, like the poor wandering dove,
I fly to the ark with my Savior to rest,
   And hear His soft whisper of love.

I cannot be weary; the days are not long,
   If onward I trustingly move;
And oft on my journey I pause in my song,
   To hear the soft
   whisper of love.

And when, from the path He has taught me to tread,
　　My footsteps forgetfully rove;
How kindly again to that path I am led,
　　And cheered by the whisper of love.

No voice in the world is so tenderly sweet,
　　No charm can my sorrow remove;
No accents in glory my joy would complete,
　　Without the soft whisper of love.

　　　　　　　　Fanny Crosby

LOOK UP!

Oh you who love the Lord,
   Look Up!
The battle has been won!
No matter what befalls you here,
"The best is yet to come!"

Though pain may rack your body,
   now,
and all earth's comforts cease,
lean on God's everlasting Arms,
and He will give you peace.

Look up beyond the shadows
   drear,
to Christ — God's shining Son,
rememb'ring that on Heaven's shore,
"The best is yet to come!"

Alice Hansche Mortenson

Within His Care

Another new day in the dawning,
Another clean slate to begin,
Another eight hours demanding
Their due in this world of men.
Another rough cross to carry,
Another steep hill to climb,
Another sweet consolation,
In placing my hand in Thine.

Another strong reason for trusting,
Another long mile to Thee,
Another deep joy in believing
Thou walkest the way with me.
Another rich harvest to gather,
Another wide field to seed,
Another dear reason to love Thee,
. . . Who knowest the things I need.

Grace E. Easley

Prayer for Faith

Before I ask, kind Father
Thou knowest of my need;
My courage faileth in the dark,
Stretch forth Thy hand to lead
My stumbling feet oe'r rugged paths;
I cannot find the way
Without the help Thou hast to give
My spirit day by day.
Almighty God, grant me to see
The working of Thy will;
May I resign myself to Thee
Retain my peace until
I trust the way Thine hand hast moved
In these affairs of mine.
Renew my faith, that I may see
Thy purposes, divine.

Anna Lee Edwards McAlpin

Where Faith Begins

Faith is the prayer
   of words unsaid,
The tear that falls upon the bed.
It is the hope of one "Amen,"
The will that trusts
   and tries again.

Faith is the day
   made fresh and new
When evening draught
   absorbs the dew.
It is the thought that lifts to bless
The one beyond the arms' caress.

It is the sky
   that leaves its gray
To welcome in a sunny day.
Faith, in a moment dares the thing
The heart petitions
God to bring.

              Roxie Lusk Smith

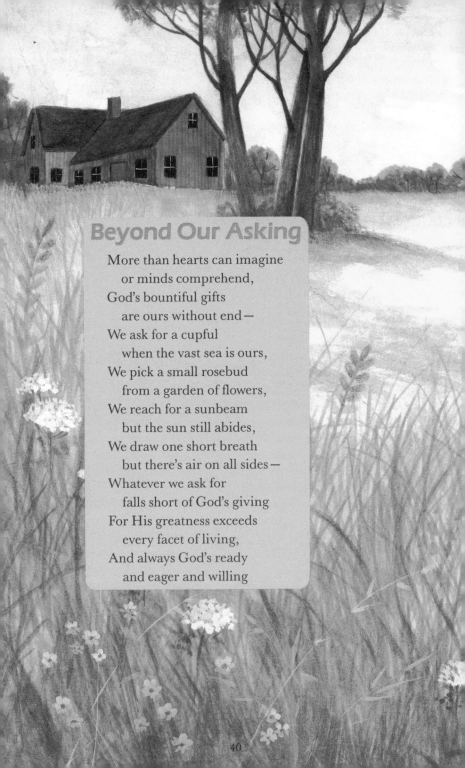

Beyond Our Asking

More than hearts can imagine
   or minds comprehend,
God's bountiful gifts
   are ours without end—
We ask for a cupful
   when the vast sea is ours,
We pick a small rosebud
   from a garden of flowers,
We reach for a sunbeam
   but the sun still abides,
We draw one short breath
   but there's air on all sides—
Whatever we ask for
   falls short of God's giving
For His greatness exceeds
   every facet of living,
And always God's ready
   and eager and willing

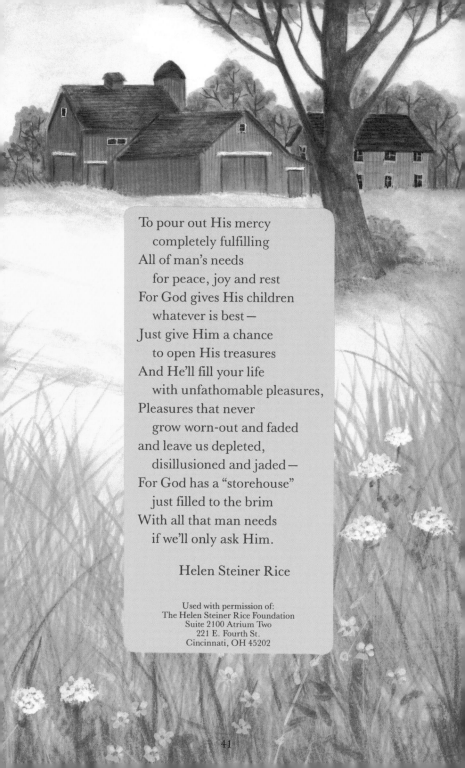

To pour out His mercy
  completely fulfilling
All of man's needs
  for peace, joy and rest
For God gives His children
  whatever is best —
Just give Him a chance
  to open His treasures
And He'll fill your life
  with unfathomable pleasures,
Pleasures that never
  grow worn-out and faded
and leave us depleted,
  disillusioned and jaded —
For God has a "storehouse"
  just filled to the brim
With all that man needs
  if we'll only ask Him.

Helen Steiner Rice

Used with permission of:
The Helen Steiner Rice Foundation
Suite 2100 Atrium Two
221 E. Fourth St.
Cincinnati, OH 45202

Love Thyself Last

Love thyself last; look near, behold thy duty
    To those who walk beside thee down life's road;
Make glad their days by little acts of beauty,
    And help them bear the burden of earth's load.

Love thyself last; look far and find the stranger
    Who staggers 'neath his sin and his despair;
Go, lend a hand and lead him out of danger
    To heights where he may see the world is fair.

Love thyself last; the vastnesses above thee
    Are filled with spirit forces, strong and pure;
And fervently these faithful friends shall love thee,
    Keep thy watch over others and endure.

Love thyself last; and thou shalt grow in spirit
    To see, to hear, to know and understand;
The message of the stars, lo, thou shalt hear it,
    And all God's joys shall be at thy command.

                    Ella Wheeler Wilcox

God's Love

To walk life alone
    takes courage.
To bend to life's needs
    takes patience.
To carry one's sorrow
    takes strength.
To live one's life
    takes faith.

To find one's courage
    takes bearing.
To find one's patience
    takes caring.
To find one's strength
    takes deep inner searching.
To find one's faith
    takes God's love.

Diana L. Crawford

Live Today

We worry needlessly at times
  Just what tomorrow brings,
We dwell on "what-if" happenings
  And other needless things.

An unkind act or word was said
  And so we sit and cry,
We dwell on hurts and sadness
  As yesterday went by.

It's now that tells the story
  So this is what I pray,
"We need your help, Dear Father,
  To live our lives today."

  Gladys Peach Anderson

Let not your heart be troubled,
Fear not; do not grieve;
Be not afraid in danger,
Trust God, in Him believe.
If you are heavy laden,
Your soul in need of rest,
Ask humbly of your Father,
You surely shall be blessed.
You know Him as your Saviour,
Your Guardian and your Friend;
You trust Him as your healer
All mercy to extend.
How sweet it is to know Him
In sunshine and in pain!
You know His promises are true,
That rainbow follows rain.

Anna Lee Edwards McAlpin

Sound of Love

Love is a power
That transforms the soul,
Fills hearts with heaven
And gives life its goal.

Loreta Inman

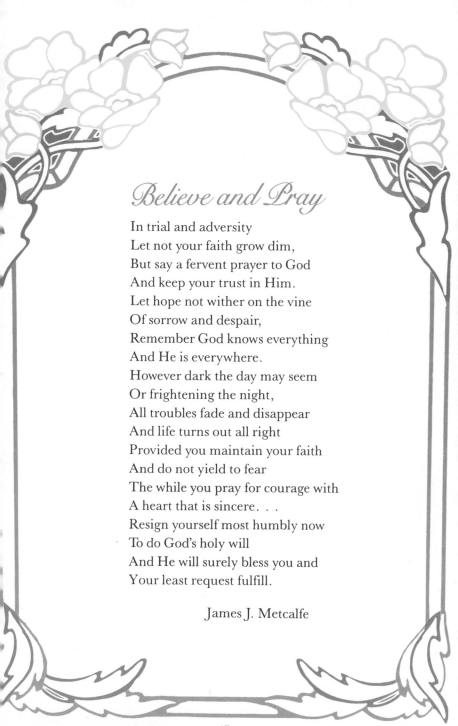

Believe and Pray

In trial and adversity
Let not your faith grow dim,
But say a fervent prayer to God
And keep your trust in Him.
Let hope not wither on the vine
Of sorrow and despair,
Remember God knows everything
And He is everywhere.
However dark the day may seem
Or frightening the night,
All troubles fade and disappear
And life turns out all right
Provided you maintain your faith
And do not yield to fear
The while you pray for courage with
A heart that is sincere. . .
Resign yourself most humbly now
To do God's holy will
And He will surely bless you and
Your least request fulfill.

James J. Metcalfe

God is Faithful

Many a grief and
Many a tear
Has been scattered over
Many a year
But this I've found:
God is faithful.

Many an injustice
Many a swat
Has the World
Given me but
God has not, because
God is faithful.

Never a burden and
Never a care
Has God allowed
For me to bear
Alone;
God is faithful.

Earth's mountains may crumble
All stars may fall
But this I know: that
Through it all
Our God reigns and
He is faithful.

Darlene R. Fountain

Dawn to Dusk

At the start of the day
Take a moment to say
A greeting to God with a prayer,
Let your thoughts fill with love
As you praise Him above
For His Fatherly ways and His care. . . .

Then all through the hours,
Through sunshine and showers,
Through smiles, as well as through tears,
In all that you do
He will stay close to you
Doubling joys and dissolving your fears. . . .

And, when the day's through
And you stop and review
Each blessing and every event,
Thank God with a prayer
For His love and His care,
And your day will end wonderfully spent!

Alice Joyce Davidson

*Y*esterday
    is already a dream
       and
Tomorrow
    is only a vision
       but
Today, well lived
    makes every
Yesterday
    a dream of happiness
       and every
Tomorrow
    a vision of
       hope.

Good Shepherd

In pastures of tender grass,
Beside waters of quietness
Thou resteth my soul.

In paths of beauty
Where only Thou couldst be,
Thou walketh beside me.

Though shadows of adversity
Should stalk my path
No evil can befall,
For Thou art ever with me.

In the midst of crowds,
Confusion, or misunderstandings,
Thou anointest me with peace;
My cup of gratitude runneth over.

So Thou art ever
Within the castle of my soul,
For Thy love and mercy
Endureth forever,
   Good Shepherd.

      Velta Myrle Allen

Open My Eyes

Open my eyes, Lord
   That I might see
The world with greater clarity.

Open my heart, Lord
   So I might learn
To care for others with more concern.

Open my ears, Lord
   And I will catch
The subtle sounds of silent distress.

And then, Lord
   Help me to be
A steadfast follower of Thee.

                    Elaine Porch

Nobody Walks Alone

Oftimes when the highway of life seems rough
   And all of your dreams have flown,
Just remember, wherever your road may go,
   Nobody walks alone.

When everyone else has let you down
   And under your sins you groan,
Just keep reminding your burdened heart,
   Nobody walks alone.

Then suddenly you'll feel His hand in yours,
   And His eyes lifting up your own,
And you'll hear His gentle, forgiving voice:
   "Nobody walks alone" . . .

Nick Kenny

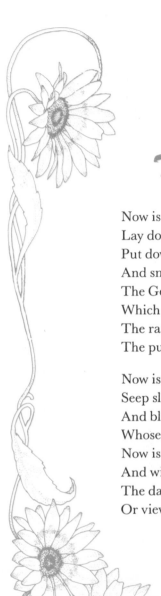

The Golden Years

Now is the time to close the books
Lay down your pen, push back your chair,
Put down the load, stretch out your feet,
And smell the flowers everywhere.
The Golden Years have now arrived,
Which seemed but just a dream before,
The rainbow's end lies just beyond
The purple hills of home, and more.

Now is the time to watch the dawn,
Seep slowly up through coral haze,
And blend your own voice with the birds,
Whose simple song is one of praise.
Now is the time to slow your steps,
And with your fingers gently trace
The dainty pattern of a leaf,
Or view a fragile snowflake's lace.

Put the work and worry down,
Now is your time beneath the sun,
The richest years within your life,
So long awaited, have begun.
The wisdom you had not in youth,
The patience that you had to earn,
The set of values you possess,
Sustain you now at every turn.

"Grow old along with me" is not
Some thoughtless phrase by witless pen,
"The very best is yet to be"
Is not just whistling in the wind.
God puts a light in every heart,
Wherein life's sweetest song is played,
And He would have us all enjoy
"The last, for which the first was made."

Grace E. Easley

Tuning

I need to go to God each day
For guidance as I go life's way;
I need the daily knowledge of
His comforting and glorious love;

As dawn awakes the birds to sing,
so praising God gives my days wing.

Pollyanna Sedziol

The Search

I sought His love in sun and stars,
And where the wild seas roll;
I found it not; as mute I stood,
Fear overwhelmed my soul;
But when I gave to one in need,
I found the Lord of Love indeed.

Thomas Curtis Clark

God's Love Lingers On

Through all the maze of all the years,
Beyond the dread and nameless fears,
Above the sorrows and the tears,
    God's love lingers on.

Past all the parting and the pain,
Through all the darkness and the rain,
Alone He stayeth just the same,
    God's love lingers on.

Through all the wickedness of sin,
Past all the noisy world of din,
Beyond the evil that's within,
    God's love lingers on.

Through all the ways and means of earth,
Beyond the pain that gives joy birth,
Above the need for happy mirth,
    God's love lingers on.

Through all the needless trial and care,
My every burden He will bear,
Through all the years I'll find Him there,
    God's love lingers on.

Through desert journey's blinding heat,
Though peace of mind I seldom meet,
O'er all the way He'll guide my feet,
    God's love lingers on.

                    Lois Tiffany

Great Hearts

The greatest heart that ever beat
Was in some patient soul
That found day's common duties sweet,
And found God makes life whole.

Loreta Inman

TRUST

Jesus, when I grow discouraged,
And the clouds alone I see,
Strengthen Thou my feeble spirit,
Give me grace to live in Thee.

Bear with me in my impatience;
Bid my restlessness to cease,
And when storms around me gather
Fill my eager heart with peace.

Not deserving of Thy caring,
In this erring life of mine,
But I know that Thou wilt guard me,
Since I am a child of Thine.

Father, bless me, and forgive me;
To the end my trust shall be
In Thy mercy, powerful ever,
To direct my soul to Thee.

    Sr. M. Electa Hampe, OSB

God's Rope

When doubts and fears assail me
And in darkness I must grope,
God sees I need Him dearly
And stretches down a dangling rope.

It stretches clear into heaven,
To its strength there is no end,
It pulls me far above the darkness
From the despair where I have been.

It wraps my wounded, bleeding heart
And fills my soul with hope,
Life's battles can never conquer
Those held securely by God's rope.

Dottlee Duggan Reid

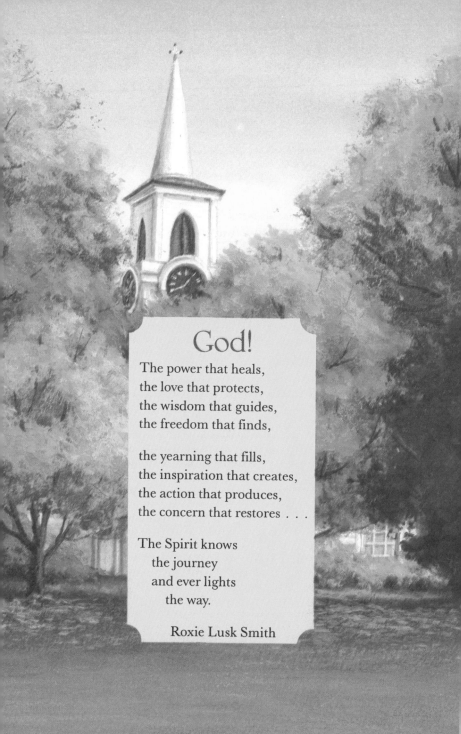

God!

The power that heals,
the love that protects,
the wisdom that guides,
the freedom that finds,

the yearning that fills,
the inspiration that creates,
the action that produces,
the concern that restores . . .

The Spirit knows
   the journey
   and ever lights
    the way.

Roxie Lusk Smith

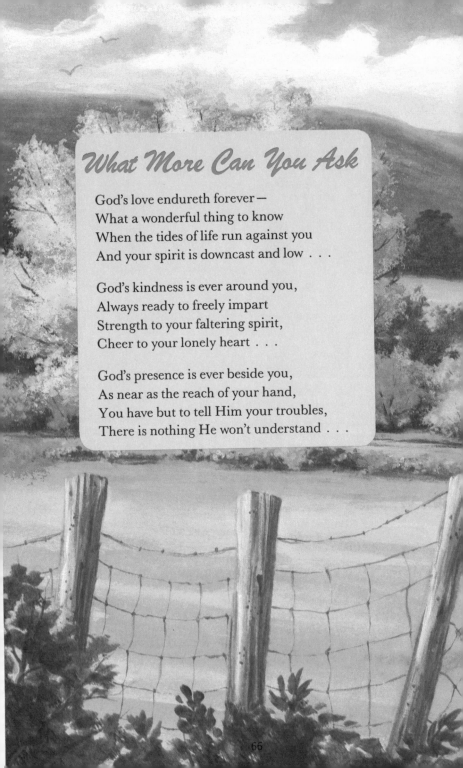

What More Can You Ask

God's love endureth forever—
What a wonderful thing to know
When the tides of life run against you
And your spirit is downcast and low . . .

God's kindness is ever around you,
Always ready to freely impart
Strength to your faltering spirit,
Cheer to your lonely heart . . .

God's presence is ever beside you,
As near as the reach of your hand,
You have but to tell Him your troubles,
There is nothing He won't understand . . .

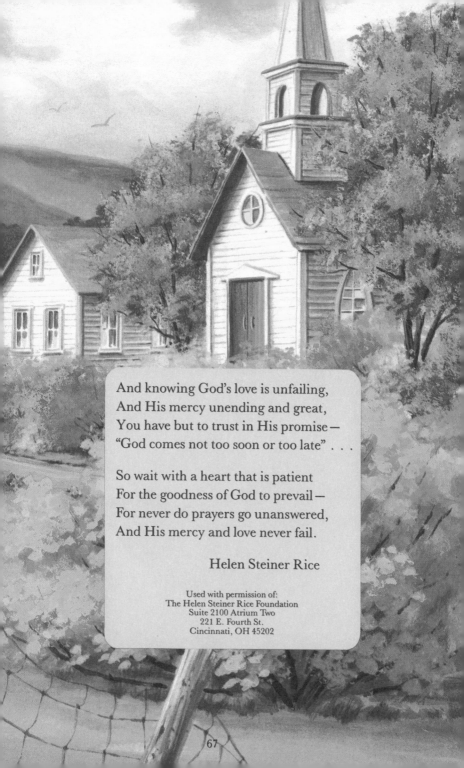

And knowing God's love is unfailing,
And His mercy unending and great,
You have but to trust in His promise—
"God comes not too soon or too late" . . .

So wait with a heart that is patient
For the goodness of God to prevail—
For never do prayers go unanswered,
And His mercy and love never fail.

Helen Steiner Rice

Used with permission of:
The Helen Steiner Rice Foundation
Suite 2100 Atrium Two
221 E. Fourth St.
Cincinnati, OH 45202

Hold On

Hold on to hope, hold on to faith
When you come to the end of the rail,
God's love is on the boundary,
He will never let you fail.

Believe in powers beyond you,
When the way is dark, without a light,
There is no place where God is not,
Even in caverns of the night.

Hold on to hope, hold on to faith,
God has a place that's just for you,
Remember that God's promises,
His love will always bring you through!

Marion Schoeberlein

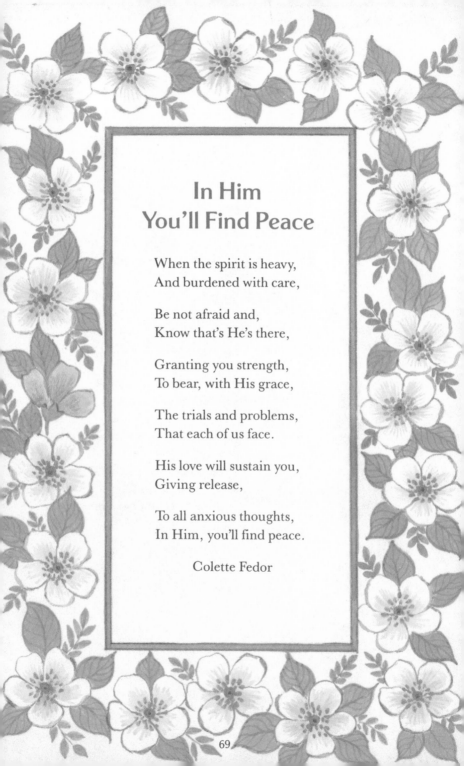

In Him
You'll Find Peace

When the spirit is heavy,
And burdened with care,

Be not afraid and,
Know that's He's there,

Granting you strength,
To bear, with His grace,

The trials and problems,
That each of us face.

His love will sustain you,
Giving release,

To all anxious thoughts,
In Him, you'll find peace.

Colette Fedor

Daybreak

Daybreak, such a precious time
God gives to you and me,
The sun breaks the horizon,
Light filters through the trees.

The dew on all the petals
Glisten so at dawn's first light,
Bursting forth in vibrant colors,
That is sure to bring delight.

God's creatures all begin the day
With such enchanting sounds,
Like the crescendo of an orchestra,
Their blend of harmony abounds.

How to see this joy and wonder
We must rise at crack of dawn,
For in the twinkling of a moment,
It will all be gone.

Albert Norman Theel

The Gentle Shepherd

Day is done and the darkness
　　Fills the earth with gloom,
I think of my many failings
　　And am fearful of my doom.

But a star shines forth in the darkness
　　And the earth is filled with light,
And I know that God's in His heaven,
　　That He guides the world aright.

And I feel that God's strong arms
　　Will keep me from my foes,
So I rest secure in His presence
　　Forgetful of life's woes.

I pray for the world so weary
　　For the sick, the poor, the old,
For I know that the gentle Shepherd
　　Will guard His own Sheepfold.

Rev. Thomas Foy

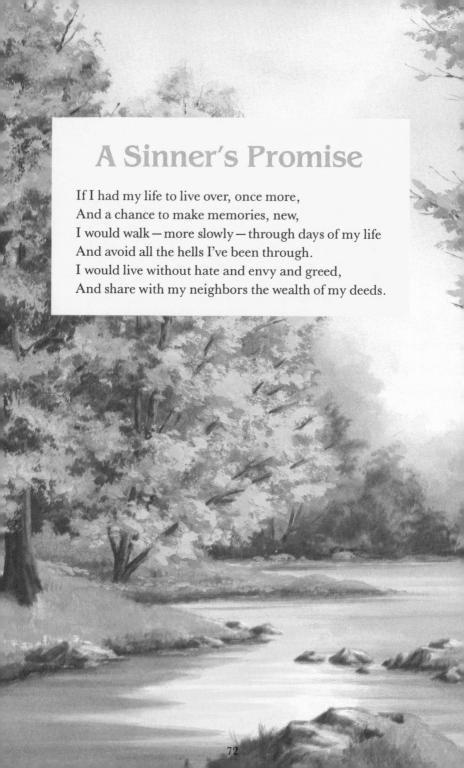

A Sinner's Promise

If I had my life to live over, once more,
And a chance to make memories, new,
I would walk — more slowly — through days of my life
And avoid all the hells I've been through.
I would live without hate and envy and greed,
And share with my neighbors the wealth of my deeds.

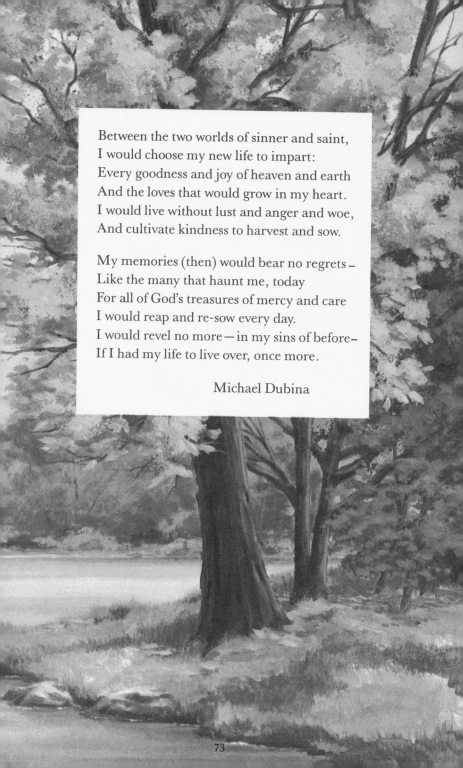

Between the two worlds of sinner and saint,
I would choose my new life to impart:
Every goodness and joy of heaven and earth
And the loves that would grow in my heart.
I would live without lust and anger and woe,
And cultivate kindness to harvest and sow.

My memories (then) would bear no regrets –
Like the many that haunt me, today
For all of God's treasures of mercy and care
I would reap and re-sow every day.
I would revel no more — in my sins of before–
If I had my life to live over, once more.

Michael Dubina

Stepping Stones

Dear Lord please always let me see
In everything befalling me,
A spark of light that I may know
That through it all You will it so.
May every silent pain I bear
Become for me a golden stair,
That rises high above the woe
Our human hearts were meant to know.

May every little heartache felt,
Each disappointment roughly dealt,
Uplift my soul that I may be
A fire that brightly burns for Thee.
And through life's waters dark and deep,
May Thy blessed presence keep
Afloat the boat in which I ride
Until I reach the other side.

For I am but a timid soul
In need of Thy dear hand to hold,
Ever trusting Thee to lend
The strength on which I can depend.
Amid the trials Thou has sent,
However plaintive my lament,
I know my tears, and sighs and groans,
Are only little stepping stones.

Grace E. Easley

Save Room in Your Heart

Find room in your heart for a stranger,
Your friends are already there,
   but there are many others who need
some love that you could spare.

Make room in your heart for the weary,
for the lost and the lonely too.
   You know — "but for the grace of God"
one of them could be you.

Each good deed becomes a seed
you plant along the way,
   and it's said — they will all come back
"tenfold" to you some day.

But the seeds you scatter all along
life's road on which you trod —
   will never grow if you don't save
some room in your heart for God!

                    Doris A. Orth

How to Find Happiness

Everybody, everywhere
  seeks happiness, it's true,
But finding it and keeping it
  seems difficult to do.
Difficult because we think
  that happiness is found
Only in the places where
  wealth and fame abound —

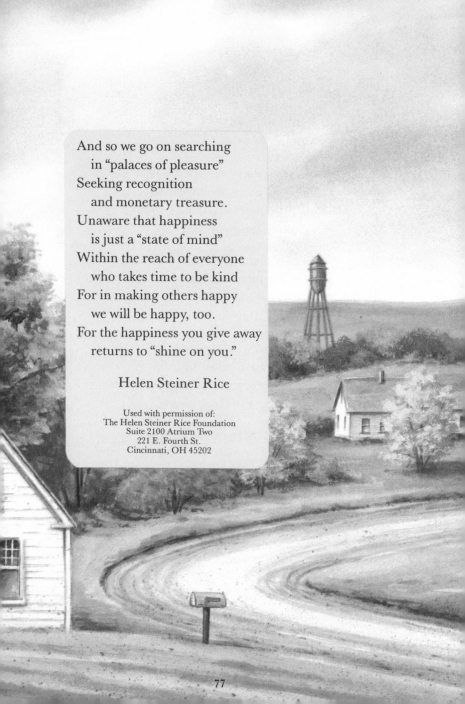

And so we go on searching
in "palaces of pleasure"
Seeking recognition
and monetary treasure.
Unaware that happiness
is just a "state of mind"
Within the reach of everyone
who takes time to be kind
For in making others happy
we will be happy, too.
For the happiness you give away
returns to "shine on you."

Helen Steiner Rice

Release

The winter winds have blown away
The sun shines warmer every day
The birds return — their song to sing
Proclaiming it is really Spring.

We breathe again, released from care,
The cold has gone we know not where
Released, we spend our time in song
The summer days are always long.

So may a soul — in loneliness
Find its release in heavenly bliss
Wrapped in the solace of truth and love
Safe in the care of God, above.

Mary Lavinia Silvia

Delay

I loved Thee late
   Too late I loved Thee, Lord,
Yet not so late
   But Thou dost still afford
The proof that Thou wilt bear
   With winning art,
One sinner more
   Upon Thy loving heart.
And may I prove,
   When all my warfare's past,
Though late I loved Thee,
   I loved Thee to the last.

       St. Augustine

Did Someone Wake At Dawn?

Did someone wake at dawn today
And think of me with love, and pray?
    I wish I knew!
For in the hour of baffling problems
    There came power.
It seemed as if His very wings
Were lifting me above the things
    That irritate.
When plans went wrong, I still could smile,
And found a song upon my lips.
With chin held high, I faced my world,
And eye to eye with truth
Moved onward through the day.
Did someone wake at dawn and pray?
    I'm sure! I know!

Carol McAfee Appleby

Thanks for Today

I do not wish for tomorrow,
for it could bring grief — or sorrow,
these few hours that I borrow
Help me live — just for today,
Grant me strength when days are dreary,
hold my hand when I am weary,
help me make some life more cheery
As I walk the Master's way.

And if I should trip — and tumble,
pick me up if I should stumble,
keep me mindful to be humble
As I journey on my way,
When my day, at last is ending
and my steps are homeward wending
with a faith in God — unending,
Thank you Jesus — for Today.

Bill Carr

Morning Prayer

Father God, Thou knowest well
the prayer within my heart,
Thank You for the chance to see
another morning start.

Touch me, Lord, with Thy sweet grace
as here I humbly pray,
Keep my loved ones in Thy sight
today and every day.

Guide my mind, my hand, my heart
in everything I do,
Grant me strength to live each day
as You would have me to.

Ask of me what Thou wouldst ask,
I'll try for all I'm worth
To do the things that You expect
with my time here on earth.

And when this day is over,
Lord bless me, that I may
live within Thy tender care
Tomorrow as today.

Ellen Abbott Pruett

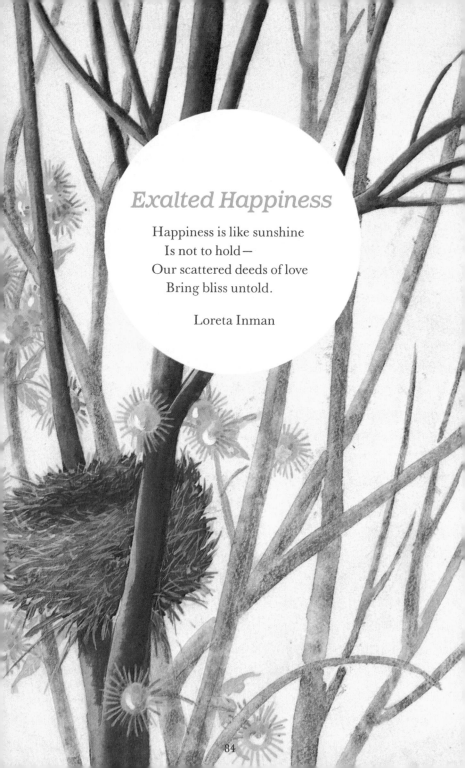

Exalted Happiness

Happiness is like sunshine
Is not to hold—
Our scattered deeds of love
Bring bliss untold.

Loreta Inman

Take Time

Take Time to think.
It is the source of power.
Take Time to play.
It is the secret of perpetual youth.
Take Time to read.
It is the fountain of wisdom.
Take Time to pray.
It is the greatest power on earth.
Take Time to love and be loved.
It is a God-given privilege.
Take Time to be friendly.
It is the road to happiness.
Take Time to laugh.
It is the music of the soul.
Take Time to give.
It is too short a day to be selfish.
Take Time to work.
It is the price of success.
Take Time to do charity.
It is the key to heaven.

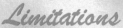

Limitations

I dedicate my trials, Lord,
my hindrances, to Thee.
My limitations grieve me now,
but someday I shall see
the Wisdom of the very things
that seem to hurt me so;
But now, within Your loving Hands
please let me glow, and grow!

Alice Hansche Mortenson

We Are All Kin

We are all kin—oh, make us kin indeed!
Spirit of Christ, we answer to Thy call
Our Father makes of us one family
One Infinite Great Love doth claim us all, —
  All one in Him!

We are all kin, though wide our various
  ways.
Spirit of Christ, that lives within all life,
Break down the barriers that time has reared,
Heal every wound and end the fruitless
  strife!

John Oxenham

Praise the Lord

Praise the Lord of all creation
As the psalmists did of old,
Sing the psalms, the songs of Sion,
In these songs God's love is told.

Search the Scriptures if you're doubtful
Of the depths of God's great love,
Proof you'll find in fullest measure,
God-inspired from above.

Give your heart to meditation
On the way you spend your days,
Then strive to make your life a poem
Fit for God's approving gaze.

Life will always have a purpose
If our model is our God
For man who's made to God's bright image
Could never rest beneath the sod.

"Come to Me," O, hear God calling,
"If your cross is hard to bear,
Give Me your love, accept My friendship,
And gladly then your cross I'll share."

Rev. Thomas Foy

88

My Worry

A little bitty worry
Started early in the day;
By noon, it seemed my worry
Hovered, standing in my way;
The things and thoughts I should have had
Got buried in my mind,
Until my little worry turned
Into the horrid kind.
By bedtime, I was frantic —
What to do, oh, what to do!
And then I couldn't go to sleep,
For worrying — fretting, too.
By morning I was almost sick,
When suddenly and soon,
My worry had been all worked out
Before the toll of noon;
Then I looked back and saw my worry
Just for what it was —
A thing that didn't happen,
As a worry seldom does.

Bonnie Daisy Nelson

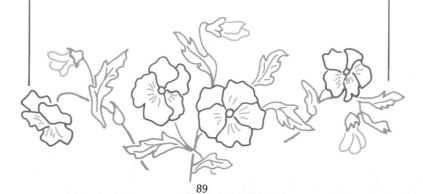

Quiet Peace

I begin and end each day with God
    What pleasure it does bring.
My heart is filled with happiness
    Lord, I have everything.

I love the quiet peace of prayer
    God gives me through the day,
And in everything I do
    I want this peace to stay.

God is peace and love and hope,
    I feel these everywhere.
I walk with God's hand in mine,
    And never know a care.

Isabel Smith

Made for God

I search for peace
In the outer courts
Where busy people
Come and go,
I search for peace
In the inner courts
With family
And those I know,
But I find peace
In the temple —
It is the Lord,
The Prince of Peace!
In Him my soul finds
Its fulfillment,
In Him alone
All longings cease.

Sr. Mary Gemma Brunke

Perfect Trust

I may not always know the way
Wherein God leads my feet.
But this I know, that round my path
His love and wisdom meet.
And so I rest content to know
He guides my feet where'er I go.

I may not always understand
Just why He sends to me
Some bitter grief, some heavy loss
But though I cannot see
I kneel and whisper through my tears
A prayer for help, and know He hears.

My cherished plans and hopes may fail,
My idols turn to dust,
But this I know: My Father's love
Is always safe to trust.
These things are dear to me, but still
Above them all I love His will.

Oh precious peace within my heart.
Oh blessed rest to know
A Father's love keeps constant watch
Amid life's ebb and flow.
I ask no more than this: I rest
Content and know His way is best.

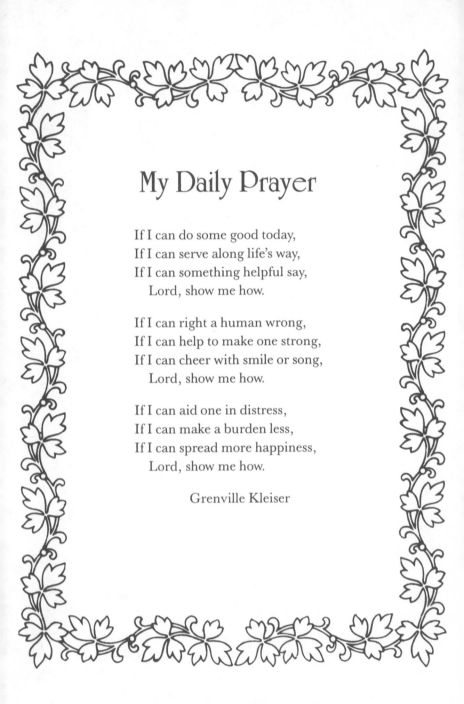

My Daily Prayer

If I can do some good today,
If I can serve along life's way,
If I can something helpful say,
   Lord, show me how.

If I can right a human wrong,
If I can help to make one strong,
If I can cheer with smile or song,
   Lord, show me how.

If I can aid one in distress,
If I can make a burden less,
If I can spread more happiness,
   Lord, show me how.

Grenville Kleiser

Love is an attitude,
  Love is a prayer
For a soul in sorrow,
  A heart in despair.

Love is good wishes
  For the gain of another.
Love suffers long
  With the fault of a brother.

Love gives water to
  A cup that's run dry.
Love reaches low
  As it can reach high.

Seeks not her own
  At expense of another.
Love reaches God
  When it reaches our Brother.

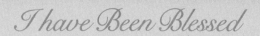

I have Been Blessed

I have been blessed far more than I deserve,
Each new day brings some cause for giving thanks,
I never could have made it all alone,
Outnumbered here among life's crowded ranks.
Had He not walked beside me all the way,
I might have missed the path obscured by weeds,
Because of Him my heart has learned to pray
Not for what it wants . . . but what it needs.

I have been blessed in countless little ways,
One of which is recognizing when,
And if He places milestones in my way,
Why 'tis to teach me how to say "Amen."

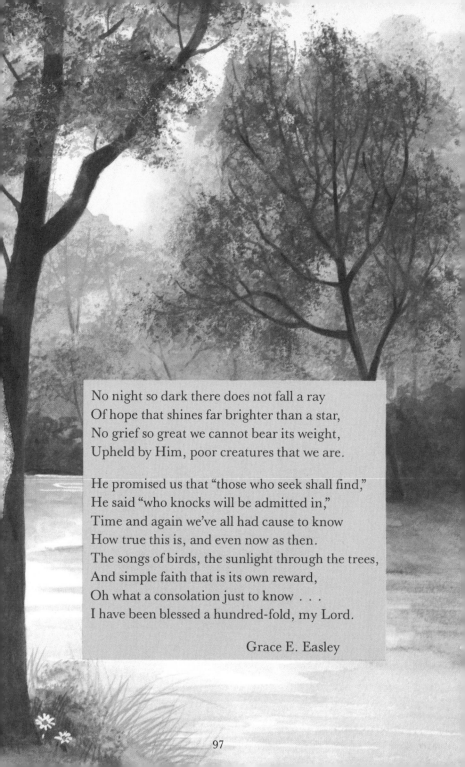

No night so dark there does not fall a ray
Of hope that shines far brighter than a star,
No grief so great we cannot bear its weight,
Upheld by Him, poor creatures that we are.

He promised us that "those who seek shall find,"
He said "who knocks will be admitted in,"
Time and again we've all had cause to know
How true this is, and even now as then.
The songs of birds, the sunlight through the trees,
And simple faith that is its own reward,
Oh what a consolation just to know . . .
I have been blessed a hundred-fold, my Lord.

Grace E. Easley

The Hand of the Heavenly Host

When broken dreams had brought me down
    so humbly on my knees,
I gathered all the faith it took
    to calm my troubled seas.

When hope seemed lost, it would return
    just when I'd need it most,
And I knew from whence it came —
    the hand of the Heavenly Host.

My strength had waned down through the years,
    too weak to rise again;
With trust, I called upon the Source —
    He whispered, "Yes, you can."

With Jesus' love supporting me
    each day my whole life through,
How can I not accomplish
    Anything I want to do.

Catherine Janssen

Sunshine and Music

A laugh is just like sunshine.
It freshens all the day,
It tips the peak of life with light,
And drives the clouds away.
The soul grows glad that hears it
And feels its courage strong.
A laugh is just like sunshine
For cheering folks along.

A laugh is just like music.
It lingers in the heart,
And where its melody is heard
The ills of life depart;
And happy thoughts come
    crowding
Its joyful notes to greet:
A laugh is just like music
For making living sweet.

God Give Me Joy

God give me joy in the common things:
In the dawn that lures, the eve that sings.

In the new grass sparkling after rain,
In the late wind's wild and weird refrain;

In the springtime's spacious field of gold,
In the precious light by winter doled.

God give me joy in the love of friends,
In their dear home talk as summer ends;

In the songs of children, unrestrained;
In the sober wisdom age has gained.

God give me joy in the tasks that press,
In the memories that burn and bless;

In the thought that life has love to spend,
In the faith that God's at journey's end.

God give me hope for each day that springs,
God give me joy in the common things!

Thomas Curtis Clark

A Little Candle

It takes no special talent,
Makes no difference who you are,
To light a little candle
That outshines the brightest star.

It doesn't call for sacrifice
To provide a little light
That might be the ray of hope
For some one thru the night.

So light up your little candle,
No matter how small the flame,
You might just get the feeling
That even you are not the same.

Clarence Bertram Dennison

O GOD, WHOSE
LOVE IS OVER ALL

O God, whose love is over all
    The children of Thy grace,
Whose rich and tender blessings fall
    On every age and place,
Hear Thou the songs and prayers we raise
    In eager joy to Thee,
And teach us, as we sound Thy praise,
    In all things Thee to see.

To see Thee in the sun by day,
    And in the stars by night,
In waving grass and ocean spray,
    And leaves and flowers bright;
To hear Thy voice, like spoken word,
    In every breeze that blows,
In every song of every bird,
    And every brook that flows.

To see Thee in each quiet home
    Where faith and love abide,
In school and church, where all may come
    To seek Thee side by side;
To see Thee in each human life,
    Each struggling human heart,
Each path by which, in eager strife,
    Men seek the better part.

John Haynes Holmes

I Have Found Such Joy

I have found such joy in simple things;
A plain clean room, a nut-brown loaf of bread,
A cup of milk, a kettle as it sings,
The shelter of a roof above my head,
And in a leaf-laced square along a floor,
Where yellow sunlight glimmers through a door.

I have found such joy in things that fill
My quiet days: a curtain's blowing grace,
A potted plant upon my window sill,
A rose fresh-cut and placed within a vase,
A table cleared, a lamp beside a chair,
And books I long have loved beside me there.

Grace Noll Crowell

Never Borrow Sorrow
From Tomorrow

Deal only with the present,
Never step into tomorrow,
For God asks us just to trust Him
And to never borrow sorrow —
For the future is not ours to know
And it may never be,
So let us live and give our best
And give it lavishly —
For to meet tomorrow's troubles
Before they are even ours
Is to anticipate the Saviour
And to doubt His all-wise powers —
So let us be content to solve
Our problems one by one,
Asking nothing of tomorrow
Except *"Thy Will be done."*

Helen Steiner Rice

Used with permission of:
The Helen Steiner Rice Foundation
Suite 2100 Atrium Two
221 E. Fourth St.
Cincinnati, OH 45202

Live With Faith

When all we own is lost to fate
And dreams have gone astray,
We learn (for first) how little we need
To live from day to day
And—from the "lightning strikes" of life—
We learn to live with grief and strife.

A truth is born of life's despairs
Whose heartaches make it known
That what we build and sow on earth
We never, truly, own;
And dreams and treasures of today,
Tomorrow's storms might sweep away.

But we must not condemn our God
For trials of land and sea
That wreck our dreams and test the loves
He willed to you and me,
It is—for us—to build, anew,
Where castles stood and flowers grew.

Our faith in God must never wane
To furies of our time.
He often lets the blossom die
To save the mother vine.
It is not meant for us to know
Which seeds we sow He means to grow.

It is — for us — to live with faith
Through calms and storms of life
And lift ourselves from our defeats,
To face each newer strife.
And, in each trial of life's despair,
To trust in God — with love and prayer.

Michael Dubina

Thy Will
Be Done

It's very difficult at times,
To face grief with a smile.
It's hard to make ourselves believe
All passes in a while.
And when the pain is sharpest,
Words seem to no avail.
When tears fall hot and heavy,
The best intentions fail.

And yet however heavy,
The burdens that we bear,
When no one else will listen,
The Lord can always hear.
When no one else will bother,
The Lord will lend a hand,
However others scorn us,
The Lord will understand.

"Life is what you make it"
Is sometimes far from true,
But the strength to keep on going,
Has got to come from you.
God promised to be with us,
And to forsake us not,
He only asks we trust in Him,
Whatever be our lot.
He only asks that we believe
He always does what's best.
To do all that we can and then
To leave to Him the rest.
Each heartache we can rise above,
Becomes a battle won,
When we can give ourselves to Him,
And say "Thy will be done".

Grace E. Easley

Endurance

Life has many ups and downs,
  The bitter and the sweet.
Each day is filled with problems
  Which tend to make us weak.

But through your faith and Jesus' love,
  You will endure the trials,
And you'll find your burdens lightened
  As you walk another mile.

Helen Parker

What God Hath Promised

God hath not promised
   Skies always blue,
Flower-strewn pathways
   All our lives through,
God hath not promised
   Sun without rain,
Joy without sorrow,
   Peace without pain.

But God hath promised
   Strength for the day,
Rest for the labor,
   Light for the way,
Grace for the trials,
   Help from above,
Unfailing sympathy,
   Undying love.

Annie Johnson Flint

Do What You Can

The smallest good deed is better by far
Than the grandest good intention.
We'll never get much accomplished in life
If our good deeds are only just mentioned.

One dollar that's given is worth much more
Than merely a promise of twenty.
For a dollar will buy a few little things,
But a promise, that won't buy any.

If we always intend to visit the sick
And don't ever put it in action,
What we plan to do won't help matters much,
And surely won't bring satisfaction.

So do what you can and give what you can
To help your less fortunate neighbor.
And you can be sure that you will receive
A very great price for your labor.

Wesley Yonts

God's Creation

The beauty of God's creation,
Is made manifest in love
His compassion is eternal
From Heaven up above.

We need only trust Him daily
To receive His Promise true
His Son gave all upon the cross
So we might live anew.

Rick Hendrickson

Never Alone

Never alone — in the darkness,
Always — His comforting hand,
Touching — so gently, with kindness,
Helping us understand.
Sharing our sorrow and sadness,
Giving us faith to believe,
With us in triumph and gladness,
Always His blessings receive.
Graciously granting forgiveness
When, for our sins we atone,
Walking beside us forever,
Leaving us never, alone.

Bill Carr

A quiet time . . .

A quiet place . . .
I seek His presence,
Know His grace.
A breathless moment;
Hours and space
Know no boundaries.
I embrace,
With my being,
Him, divine.
I am His . . . and
He is mine.

Anna Lee Edwards McAlpin

Somebody's Smile

Somebody smiled and the load I bore,
lighter became than ever before.
The road ahead wasn't nearly as long,
and soon I was singing a joyful song.
Hearing the song, another drew near,
whose heart was anxious and full of fear.
We communed awhile of heavenly things,
till doubt and misgivings had taken wings.
Then each to his task with a prayer and a song,
and a smile on our lips to help others along.
How many were helped? We'll know after while.
but it all began with somebody's smile!

Alice Hansche Mortenson

God's Touch of Wonder

Dawn tenderly touches the darkened earth
Night shadows silently melt away
Then the sun bursts over the horizon
God's touch of wonder displayed.

Dew drops dance and glisten like diamonds
Dawn's brilliance cannot be contained
Morning glories proudly unfold their splendor
God's touch of wonder sustained.

A sparrow soars til the clouds engulf him
Then descends to sing me his songs
Of dawn and a new beginning
God's touch of wonder to me belongs.

As the miracle of dawn is unfolding
In awe and humility I pray
For awareness of warmth, song, and splendor of
God's touch of wonder . . . today!

Dorothy Leonard Sharpe

Waymarks

I do not ask that God reveal
The "why" of things to me.
I do not ask that He explain,
   Or pardon what I see.

I do not ask to see results
Before I can believe;
When things are masked, a larger faith
   Would ask and then receive.

But this I ask — when moods are weak,
   When prayers seem lost, unheard,
My soul be fortified the more
   To take God at His word.

When days come on with partial suns,
And shadows move with pain,
My heart be lifted, healed to know
I do not trust in vain.

                    Roxie Lusk Smith

This I Know

He gives me faith
to persevere
though life's storms
hover near.

His hand takes mine
and holds it tight;
I cling to Him
with all my might.

He alone
can help me cope;
He alone
can give me hope.

There's no one else
so strong as He;
In storms of life
He strengthens me.

He gives support
when rough winds blow;
He's always there
This I know.

Jeri Sweany

All's Well

My heart,
 The sun hath set.
Night's paths
 With dews are wet.

Sleep comes
 Without regret;
Stars rise
 When sun is set.

All's well.
 God loves thee yet,
Heart, smile,
 Sleep sweet, nor fret.

William A. Quayle

God's Love

We call it mercy —
   It is God's forgiving love.
We call it providence —
   It is God's caring love.
We call it kindness —
   It is God's understanding love.
We call it Christ's passion and death —
   It is God's proven love.
We call it happiness —
   It is God's encouraging love.
We call it the will of God —
   It is God's unerring love.
We call it heaven —
   It is God's rewarding love.
We call it eternity —
   It is God's unending love.

Sr. Mary Gemma Brunke

Always Near You

When you go to church on Sunday
Though you know He's everywhere,
Don't you feel that more than ever
God is really, truly there?
Isn't there a certain something
In that solemn atmosphere,
That inspires you to thinking
God is somewhat extra near?
Don't you hear the angels singing
When you listen to the choir,
And don't all your good intentions
Rise at least a little higher?
Yes, of course, you have that feeling,
But it is not church on Sunday,
For that's just a time for worship
You would seldom take on Monday.
You could always be inspired
If you spoke to God each day,
And remembered every moment
He is never far away.

James J. Metcalfe

Trust God

There's never a teardrop
  that God doesn't see.
He knows when a sparrow
  falls from a tree.
There's never a moment
  when God doesn't care
Never a time when He
  won't hear our prayer.

Patricia Emme

He Cares

Oh, wonderful story of deathless love;
Each child is dear to that Heart above.
He fights for me when I cannot fight,
He comforts me in the gloom of night,
He lifts the burden, for He is strong,
He stills the sigh and awakes the song;
The sorrow that bows me down He bears,
And loves and pardons, because He cares.

Let all who are sad take heart again;
We are not alone in our hours of pain;
Our Father stoops from His throne above
To soothe and quiet us with His love.
He leaves us not when the storm is high,
And we have safety, for He is nigh.
Can it be trouble that He doth share?
Oh, rest in peace, for the Lord doth care!

Susan Coolidge

Make Me a Channel, Lord!

Let me be a channel, Lord,
Through which Your love can flow.
Where I find darkness, let me bring
A warm and hopeful glow.
Help me, Lord, bring faith and trust
Where I find misbelief,
And let me wipe the tears that come
with sorrow, hurt, and grief.
Help me find the way, Lord,
To find new channels, too,
Through which Your love can flow until
The world is one with You!

Alice Joyce Davidson